The Terrible Twos 2

Compiled by Sarah Kennedy

The Terrible Twos 2

This book is published to accompany
BBC Children in Need
televised and broadcast in November 1998

First published in 1998
by BBC Worldwide Limited
80 Wood Lane London W12 0TT

ISBN 0 563 55531 9

Printed and bound in Great Britain by
Butler and Tanner Limited, Frome

Laminated cover printed by
Lawrence Allen Limited, Weston-super-Mare

**Every copy sold includes a 50p donation
to the 1998 BBC Children in Need Appeal.**

Sarah Kennedy and BBC Worldwide have made every effort
to contact the contributors to this book. Should they have failed
to do so, they will be pleased to correct this at the earliest
possible opportunity.

Hello again!

I cannot believe it's four years since, between us, we cobbled together *Terrible Twos 1*. My new little friend Molly's comment started the ball rolling when she frantically dug up the nasturtium seeds we'd planted 30 minutes previously, thinking that because they hadn't come up yet, they'd 'got lost'.

As I write this, a phone call has come in from her mother Jude in Australia informing us all on Radio 2's *Dawn Patrol* that Molly is now learning Japanese and has a 'PUTER'!

You have continued to contribute all your personal stories and not a day passes without my BBC mail reflecting the wonderful way the Terrible Twos see life. They have the ability to cut through the rubbish and there is a frightening truthfulness about their utterances. They also have the ability to shame, embarrass, create laughter, tears, huge love and, if you are a hypocrite, you'd better duck for cover!

Children in Need 1998 is looming as I write this little introduction and it seemed right once again to slip your input between a new set of covers. Hopefully we can repeat the huge sum of money *Terrible Twos 1* contributed to Radio 2's cheque to this wonderful BBC charity.

Shooting the cover of this book was not a piece of cake. Understatement. May Corfield has done a wonderful 'editing' job and, as I really wanted a young man on the cover, and as we'd had a young lady on the previous cover, could we borrow May's young son Thomas? He brought his friend Megan. Now young Megan oozed into the camera, eagerly climbing onto my completely strange lap. She was wonderful, totally unfazed by camera boxes, light reflectors and the usual paraphernalia of a photo shoot. Thomas – you must be joking! A young man with attitude! May visibly squirmed when he looked me straight in the eye and announced:

'I don't like you. I don't like your house and I'm *not* sitting on your knee. I want my Smarties and I want to go home to my house!'

He'll be OK if he learns to speak his mind! In the end we managed to get two of our wriggling monsters looking good. You can always airbrush the old bat in the middle!

Thank you all again for 'doing your bit' for Children in Need – nudge, nudge – the book makes a good Christmas or Easter present!

Listener Diane Claridge has the last word:

'Last year I bought a copy of your novel, *Charlotte's Friends*. One morning when I was getting dressed, my daughter Laura looked at the photograph on the back of the book and said, "Is that Sarah Kennedy?"

"Yes," I replied.

"What, that lady who is talking on the radio now?"

"Yes," I replied again, "why?"

"Because she sounds like she's got black hair on the radio!" '

Happy Days. Happy Reading.

Sarah Kennedy

My beautiful laundry

My granddaughter, Charity, was nearly three when she went to visit her newly-married Auntie Vanessa. The rear garden was visible from the road and Charity, strapped in her car seat, craned her neck to see. Excitedly, she exclaimed at the top of her voice, 'Oh, Nanna!' followed by a long pause. 'Auntie Vanessa has a new washing line'. Then there was a big sigh, followed by: 'Isn't it beautiful!'

Marion (Nanna) Maddox

Fame at last

My granddaughter Jessica suffers with cystic fibrosis and has been in the Brompton Hospital many times. About two years ago the *Daily Mirror* published photos of Princess Diana visiting the children there. It was a great surprise to see our granddaughter's photo on the front page, sitting next to Diana.

When Jessica arrived home from school that day, her Mum said, 'How did you get on today, Jessica?' The reply came: 'I'm fed up being famous!'

Molly Waugh

Hippy-chippy

A few years ago when my daughter Grace was about three, we went to the local chip shop for a take-away. On our arrival, we had to join an already extremely long queue.

Everyone was waiting patiently and quietly when, suddenly, the door opened and in walked a middle-aged hippy-looking chap. He had long, wavy blonde hair and a beard, and was wearing a canvas cloak and sandals on his feet. My daughter's face lit up in wonderment, and she grabbed my arm and proclaimed loudly and clearly, 'Daddy, look!! There's Jesus!'

Chris Dale

Feeling the pinch

Our niece Ruth has a very bright two-year-old girl called Rebecca, who was having trouble accepting her new baby brother, Dan. One day Ruth left the two of them alone in the living room.

Alerted by terrible crying from the baby, Ruth rushed in. He was very upset and she looked carefully to see if there was a nappy pin sticking into him. Finding no obvious reason for his distress, she said, 'Do you know why he's crying, Rebecca?'

There was a pause, then Rebecca said, 'Maybe somebody pinched him.'

Sandra Bradley

Birthday logic

When my niece Georgina was just two, I took her to see Father Christmas in Norfolk.

Father Christmas: 'What's your name?'
Georgina: 'Georgie.'
Father Christmas: 'How old are you?'
Georgina: 'Two.'
Father Christmas: 'And when were you two?'

Georgina *(with suitably scathing look):* 'On my birthday.'

Christine Walker

"ANY MORE STUPID QUESTIONS?"

Young love

Our grandson Edward, aged seven, has a friend called Dale, also seven, who lives across the road. One day Edward said to his Mum, 'Dale's got a girlfriend.'

'Oh, how nice,' said his Mum, 'have you got one?' There was a long pause, then Edward said, 'Well, there is a girl who loves me, but I'm not going to rush it.'

Myrtle Tarr

Wee Willie Winkie

While relieving myself in the bathroom, my son Thomas, aged three, rushed in, red in the face, saying, 'Daddy, Daddy, I need to do a wee-wee!'

With that, he pulled down his shorts and did his wee right there alongside me! We both stood there looking like a pair of garden fountains.

When Thomas had finished, he looked up at me, looked down at himself, up at me again and said, 'Daddy, I've got a small winkle,' pausing only to add a moment later, 'and so have you!'

Dean Morgan

Egg head

Many years ago when I was serving in the RAF in Cyprus, my wife took my son, then aged three, to see the SSAFA nurse as there had been a reported outbreak of head lice at his playschool. The nurse was a rather confused old dear who examined his head and proclaimed him clear.

After several days, he was still complaining of an itchy head, so we examined him ourselves and found one of the little blighters! A trip to the station medical centre followed and the family were all advised to use a special shampoo. A few days later my wife and son were in a checkout queue in the crowded NAAFI shop and who should be beside them but the SSAFA nurse. My son said something to her about eggs but she said, 'No, dear, it's not Easter now!' to which our exasperated little son shouted at the top of his voice, 'I've got eggs in my head!'

The poor nurse went off speechless, leaving her shopping behind!

B. E. Collis

The Terrible Twos 2

Kerb crawler!

My husband is a driving instructor and when I am out walking with my granddaughter Leah, aged three, we often see him on a driving lesson. One day when I was looking after Leah, we had the following conversation:

Leah: 'Where's Grandad?'
Me: 'He's working.'
Leah: 'Why?'
Me: 'To earn some pennies.'
Leah: 'No, he isn't.'
Me: 'What's he doing then?'
Leah: 'Picking up ladies.'

Sandra Bower

Bicycle love

Mummy was in the kitchen preparing dinner.

Jack: 'Mummy, what do you know about girls?'
Mum: 'Quite a lot, Jack. Why?'
Jack: 'I've decided when I grow up I'm going to marry Alison and Jane.'
Mum: Well, you'll only be able to marry one of them, Jack, so you'd better decide which one you prefer.'

Jack sat down at the kitchen table and thought.

Jack: 'Mummy, I've decided.'
Mum: 'So, who is it going to be then?'
Jack: 'Jane.'
Mum: 'Why Jane?'
Jack: 'She's got a better bike.'

Anon

Funny bone

I had just knitted a jumper for my grandson, Andrew, with Power Rangers on the front. Knowing that it was rather long on him, I asked him if it fitted him when he phoned up to thank me.

'Yes,' he said, 'but it comes down to the elbows on my legs.'

Scotland Granny

Busy Santa

At the school Christmas Fair our grandson Ronan, aged six, told Santa what he would like for Christmas. His parents were horrified as there were some things not on the original list.

A few days later his Mum took him to see Santa in Kingston. When it was Ronan's turn, he went to Santa and said, 'I can see you are busy and, as I only saw you a couple of days ago, I won't take up any more of your time,' and walked off leaving Santa speechless!

Grandad Kitchin

I-spy

One day we were playing I-spy and Jordy, aged four, said it was something beginning with 'M'. We all guessed different things for some time. Eventually we gave up. Jordy then held up the TV remote control and triumphantly said, 'It's a Mote control, of course!'

Anon

Getting to know you

My grandson Adam was never a 'cuddly' baby. When he was three he was sitting on his mother's knee and he let her cuddle him. She told him, 'When you were a baby, Adam, you would never let me cuddle you.' Looking up at her, he replied, 'You know Mummy, I didn't know you very well then.'

Nana Gladys Collins

Long live the King!

After watching the Queen and Prince Philip on television, there was a rather amusing conversation between my daughter, Claire, and my granddaughter, Sarah.

Sarah: 'Mum, who's the King of England?'

Mum: 'We don't have a King, Sarah. We have a queen who is Queen Elizabeth.'

Sarah: 'Who is the Queen married to, then?'

Mum: 'She's married to Prince Philip.'

Sarah: 'Well,' replied Sarah, 'why isn't he King if he's married to the Queen?'

Mum: 'Because the Queen is in charge and her husband is her assistant.'

Sarah: 'So Queen Elizabeth is Queen and Prince Philip is her husband but not a King?'

Mum: 'Yes, Sarah, that's right.'

Sarah: 'So, we definitely don't have a King?'

Mum: 'No, Sarah, we don't.'

After a couple of minutes thought, Sarah then piped up: 'Well, if we don't have a King, who is Elvis?'

Clive Lambshead and Sarah Fennell

His and hers

One day I had a phone call from the department store John Lewis, to advise me on the date of a delivery. Jack, my five-year-old, answered the phone in his most grown-up voice, then looked most puzzled. Calling for me, he yelled, 'She says it's John Lewis, but I think it's really his wife!'

Heather Hillcox

Looking for God

When my grandson was three and a half, he went on his first trip in a plane flying over the Atlantic. He started running up and down the aisle, frantically looking out of the windows, so his mother, getting a little cross, said, 'Julian, come and sit down! What are you doing?'

'I'm looking for God, but I can't see him.'

Margaret Philipps-Thomas

The dentist's chair

When my son Alan was small, I took him to the dentist for a check-up. The dentist examined his teeth and said he needed a tiny filling, which he did straight away.

When he had finished, he said to Alan, who was still lying back in the chair: 'Spit that out.'

Alan did as he was told, and just propelled the water straight out of his mouth! After composing himself, the dentist said, 'Well, I suppose I asked for that!'

Jill Pulford

Clean sweep

Jak, my grandson, was staying with me during the school holidays when he was six. He loved helping me around the house with the sweeping and dusting. One day a friend called in for a cup of tea and she saw Jak with his broom.

'What a good boy you are, helping your Nan!' she said. 'He's just like his Mummy,' I said. 'She's always so tidy.'

Jak than piped up, 'Excuse me, Nanny, which corner should I sweep it into?'

Eileen Collins

God-given

My brother once belonged to the local Horticultural Society. One year the local nursery and primary school were having a Harvest Festival and he was invited to attend the service.

All the little children trooped into the assembly hall carrying the gifts of food and produce which were later distributed to the old folk. During the service, the head teacher told the story of the loaves and fishes. Coming to the end of the tale, she said, 'Although we haven't any fish here today, we mustn't forget that God provides the fish for us to eat.' All was quiet for a second or two, then a little voice from among the children piped up, 'But Miss, I brought a tin of salmon.'

Cynthia Davies

Cowgirl

Andrew and Jane were watching a programme on children's TV which involved a visit to a farm. I went into the room to find them glued to the screen watching a cow giving birth to a calf. They were so engrossed that they didn't notice their Mummy standing behind them.

When the cow eventually gave birth, Jane turned to Andrew and said, 'Did Mummy have us like that when she was a cow?'

Gillian Harper

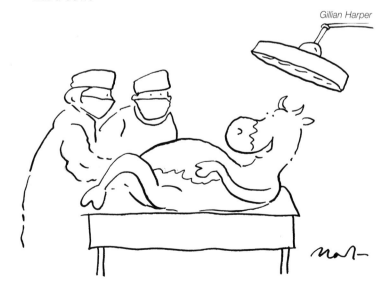

Now wash your hands!

After having my children, I returned to nursery teaching at a local school, assisting the nursery teacher. On the very first day, I took a boy along to the loo and was very pleased to see him go straight to the basin to wash his hands afterwards.

'Oh, you are a good boy,' I said, in my best Joyce Grenfell voice.

He replied innocently, 'Mummy says you must always wash your hands because there are Germans in the loo.'

As you can imagine, I had a mental picture of an Herr Flick character climbing out over the seat!

Elaine (Maggi) Delaney

Tenor trouble

One day I was trying in vain to watch The Three Tenors, but my daughter Eleanor, aged three, had other ideas. I tried to explain that they were very famous singers and that it was a very special concert. At that moment, the great Placido Domingo began to sing.

Eleanor: 'He sang that one before.'
Me: 'No, he didn't.'
Eleanor: 'Well … does he know Twinkle, Twinkle Little Star, then?'

Anon

Horsing around

I was at Wetherby races on Easter Monday, standing by the paddock watching the horses parading before the last race. A little girl was standing next to me with her mother.

While parading, one of the horses defecated copiously right in front of us. The little girl regarded the steaming heap in silence for a moment and then said, 'At least it smells better than Daddy's.'

Anon

The Terrible Twos 2

Now if anyone knows anything about Terrible Twos, it has to be Sheelah Evans. She sent me these two stories – look out for three more later on! SK

Tied up

I run a kindergarten in Shoeburyness, Essex, with about 90 two-and-a-half to four-year-olds. One day the school secretary came into the classroom with a message during storytime. 'Mrs Evans, I have a message from your husband. I'm afraid he won't be able to collect your children tonight as he's been tied up at work.'

Tara, with her eyes wide open and shocked face, said, 'Mrs Evans, who's tied up your husband?'

Ain't misbehaving

I know that manners and other things I have taught the children at kindergarten have really registered when I hear comments like the following:

Guy: 'Mrs Evans, I ain't got no red!' holding up the pencil pot.

Me: 'Oh Guy, we don't say that do we… what do we say?'

Guy *(after a moment in thought):* 'I ain't got no black!'

Morning cuppa

When Joanne was seven, she appeared at the bedroom door early one Sunday morning carrying a tray with two mugs on. 'I've made you and Daddy a cup of tea,' she said. I was shocked, as she was not allowed to use the kettle, but I didn't want to upset her as she seemed so proud of herself. I thanked her, took a sip and immediately spat it across the room. It was lukewarm and had a very strange taste, so I asked how she had made it.

'I know you said I couldn't use the kettle,' she said, 'but my hot water bottle was still warm so I used the water from that!'

Pam James

Video heaven

Our grandson Billy is four and my father was 84 when he died in March this year. So that Billy could differentiate between us, my father was known as Old Grandad and I am simply Grandad. His great grandparents had bought Billy a video to watch whenever he visited them.

Recently, while chatting to his Mum, Billy said, 'When Old Grandad died, did he go to heaven?' 'Yes,' said his Mummy.

'And when Old Nanny dies, will she go to heaven as well?' 'Yes,' replied his Mummy, 'so that she can be with Old Grandad.'

After a long pause, Billy said, 'And will she take the Popeye video with her when she goes?'

Tony Spring

Brain-teaser

About a year or so ago, it was announced on the news that female brains were bigger than male brains. My daughter heard her sons discussing this in the car. Sam, aged eight, said, 'How can they be bigger, because men are bigger than women?' Joshua, aged six, replied, 'Mummies need bigger brains because they can do more jobs at once!'

Pat Dance

Witch book?

When he was small, I took my son Jamie to the library. He selected his six books and took them to the counter to be stamped by the librarian. In a loud, clear voice that only a three-year-old could muster, he said, 'Oh, Mummy! Isn't she kind letting me have all these books and she looks just like a witch, doesn't she?'

Joanna Mair

Gone bananas

When I was in the Royal Marines, I was on leave and visited my sister Cheryl in Eastbourne. My niece Annalie, then four, came scrambling towards me, all girlish shrieks and flailing arms. Full of excitement at seeing her wandering uncle again, she started to tell me everything she had seen or heard in the last few days — all in one breath!

As she calmed down, she looked at me smugly and said, 'Uncle Kevin, I can spell banana ...'

Then her face fell and she looked crestfallen as she continued, 'but I don't know when to stop!'

The thought of 'banananananananana' has stayed with me ever since!

"HOW MANY 'NANAS' IN BANANA ?"

Kev Barnes

Flying pigs

When our son David, aged three, had just started nursery school, he came home to lunch one day with his big sister Lynne, aged six.

David: 'I know where wool comes from!'

Lynne: 'No, you don't!'

David: 'Yes, I do!'

Lynne: 'Where?'

David: 'Well, first you take the feathers off the pig!'

Janet and Burt Chatwin

Hand it over!

My grandson Tom, aged four, was fascinated when told that his new friend's family celebrated 'Passover' instead of Easter, as they are Jewish.

A little later, the topic of Easter arose again and Tom joined in the conversation, announcing that his friend doesn't have Easter — 'He has Handover.'

Patricia Aspinall

Birds and bees

I lost my wife at the early age of 27 and found myself alone with four-year-old twins to bring up. One day I was confronted by a very serious Samantha.

'Daddy, Mrs Canter has just had a baby girl.' I told her I already knew.

'It was in her tummy.' I told her I knew that too.

'How did it get there?' she asked.

I had long decided that, when the moment came, I would tell it like it was and get it over and done with. So I went into an explanation I thought was suitable for her, but was as graphic as I thought fitting.

When I had finished, there was a long silence and then:

'Well, if you're going to be silly, I'll ask Auntie Mabbs!'

Anon

Sibling rivalry

When our second child was born and, despite carefully obeying the teachings of Dr Spock (as one did in 1965), our first child Sara was very jealous. She was then two and a quarter. It became very worrying when she used to wake in the wee hours, patter across the landing and belt baby Jonathon with her Barbie doll!

Out for a drive one day, Jonathon was grizzling in his Moses basket.

'Why do we have to have him?' asked Sara, 'Why don't we throw him away?'

Hoping to call her bluff, my husband hit the brakes and said, 'Shall I throw him over the hedge?' There was no reply from Sara, so my husband stopped the car and reached for the Moses basket.

'No, no!' shouted Sara, 'Don't throw him away!'

We exchanged glances, thinking that Sara did love her brother after all. The relief was short-lived as Sara continued: 'Take his clothes off first — they'll fit my rabbit!'

Jill Dean

Rainbow woe

It had been a particularly heavy night of rain, but we woke to a bright morning and my wife decided to take our daughter, then three, to the shops in her pushchair. En route, she had to pass by the local garage.

As they were passing, quite suddenly and unexpectedly, our daughter burst into tears. 'Stop! Stop! Stop Mummy!' she sobbed. Alarmed at this unusual outburst, my wife stopped and bent down to comfort her. 'What's the matter darling?' she asked. 'Oh look, Mummy!' she sobbed, pointing to a puddle on the garage forecourt, which was covered in a thin but colourful oily film, 'A dead rainbow!'

John from Hampshire

Egg timer

When my granddaughter Laura was about three or four, the children at her playschool were told the story of Jesus. It was Easter time and one evening when her Mum was bathing her, Laura asked, 'Mummy, when did Jesus die?'

'He died on Good Friday,' replied her Mum. 'And when did he rise again?' came the next question. 'On the third day after Easter Sunday,' said her Mum. Laura paused, deep in thought, and then said, 'Just in time for his Easter eggs.'

Joan Stanway

Aping about

A friend of mine was talking to her daughter one day, who said, 'Mummy, you know we are all descended from the Apes?'

'Yes,' replied her mum.

'Well, is that on Daddy's side or your side?'

Jane Fox

Welsh pasta

When Dyfrig was six (and also bilingual) I asked him what his favourite food was, and went through the list: chips, baked beans, cake? It was none of those.

Dyfrig was thinking hard and said, 'I don't know the English name for it, only the Welsh name — LASAGNE.'

Cherie Cresswell

In the dark

When my youngest daughter was about four, we lived on a small farm at Hythe in Kent. I wanted to buy a torch with a good beam so I could see the sheep at night during lambing time, so I took Sylvie with me to an electrical shop.

The young man who served me was very helpful and even asked me if I wanted to go into the back room to shine the torch to make sure the beam was strong enough. I said as a joke, 'I'm not going in the dark with you!' not thinking that Sylvie was listening intently.

A few days later, I went back to the shop for something else. It was quite crowded and Sylvie spotted the same young man and piped up: 'That's the man who wanted to take you into the dark.'

Daphne Beatrice Hollands

Rub-a-dub-dub

My four-year-old grandson was having his bath before bedtime, together with plastic boats, buckets and Action Man swimming around looking for sharks.

I picked up the sponge, saying, 'I wish I had someone to wash my back when I'm in the bath,' to which he replied, 'You should do the same as my Daddy — he has a big scrubber to do his back.' There's no answer to that!

Rita Rabassa

The Terrible Twos 2

Over and out

Natasha, aged three, and I were playing with her 'toy of the day' — a set of two mobile phones. To liven it up a bit, I began ending each conversation with 'over and out'.

Natasha soon cottoned on and the following dozen or so calls all finished with the now obligatory words, until the very last message, which was followed by a pregnant pause and then an exasperated, 'Well, are you coming over, or are you going out?'

Mary Mansfield

Mouldy old gran!

When my granddaughter Hannah was two, my mother, whom she calls 'GG' (for Great Grandma) had a fall and bumped her face. She cut her eyelid and needed stitches, which caused very bad bruising.

A few days after the accident I asked her if she would like to come and visit my granddaughter and she agreed, as long as I thought her face wouldn't frighten Hannah. When we arrived, Hannah opened the door, everybody said hello and nothing about GG's face was mentioned. However, I couldn't help feeling that something was going to happen.

About three hours later, Hannah was bouncing on her trampoline and she turned to me, without taking an extra breath and said, 'Why has GG's face gone mouldy?'

P. A. Kyle

Brain power

I was once babysitting for a friend's grandchildren. Timothy, then four, showed me his school work and was very proud of his gold star for spelling. He said he had some homework to do at the weekend and I asked him what it was.

'I've got to read a book and then write about it, but I can't do it now as I have to be in bed by 8 o'clock.' I suggested that he read the book before bed and then write about it the following day. His reply was, 'But Sue, my brain isn't big enough to remember yesterday, and today will be yesterday tomorrow, won't it?'

Sue Taylor

Give us a clue

About twelve years ago my two boys were playing hide and seek in the garden. Nick, aged three, had been hidden for some time and Matthew, aged two, was getting frustrated.

Matt: 'I can't find you. Give me a clue.'

Nick: 'I'm in the shed!'

Christine Taylor

Motor mouth

When my son Michael was about four, he used to talk constantly, engaging in conversation and questioning everything. At the time I had a four-month-old baby to look after and, on one particularly tiring day when the baby was being fractious, in utter frustration I said, 'Oh, Michael! For goodness sake, will you shut up!'

His reply came: 'Well, Mummy, I can't help it — my voice is so full of words!'

Jessie Statham

Battery operated

Our granddaughter Stephania, nearly six, was looking out of the airport terminal window at an aircraft with its underbelly hatch open in readiness to receive luggage:

'Mummy, is that where they put the batteries?'

Anthony D. Humphries

The Terrible Twos 2

Comedy of manners

Our two-year-old niece Charlotte visits us most weekends with her mother, who is teaching her to say 'Thank you for having me' when she leaves. On a recent visit, as they were leaving, her mother duly said to her, 'And what do you say?'

Charlotte, very pleased with herself, came out with the obligatory 'Thank you.'

'And what else?' asked Mum.

Charlotte thought for a moment, then the light dawned.

'Can I have a packet of crisps before I go?'

Chris Sharp

Peas in our time

My niece Chloe, aged six, had been listening to the news on the radio with her mother and had obviously been taking it all in. Later on, she asked, 'Mum, why are they always talking about Irish Pea-Stalks?'

Zarla Harriman

In the bag!

My granddaughter Charlotte, aged four, on her first rough Channel crossing on a ferry said to her Mum, 'Mummy, why are all these grown-ups shouting into paper bags?'

Marjorie McTighe JP

Papal surprise

On Pauline's christening day, we all arrived at the packed church. All went quiet, but as the vicar was about to begin, my young son Nick broke the silence with: 'When is the Pope arriving?'

S. Hopper

Dalek shock

Many years ago I was on a crowded bus. As we came to a bus stop, a little boy standing at the front looking through the window suddenly shouted out, his voice full of alarm: 'Mum, Mum! Look Mum! Daleks! Daleks!'

Everyone on the bus craned their heads to see and there, gliding towards us, were two nuns!

Michael F. Williams

Designer kids

My daughter Louise was out shopping with her three children, Thomas, aged six, Lauren, five, and Caitlin, 20 months. They were in the menswear department looking at jeans.

Thomas, who reads everything in sight, announced that Louise could have called him Ralph, Lauren could still be Lauren and Caitlin could be Easyfit!

Micky Crerar

Golden winkle

Recently we were staying with some friends in Kent and had a visit to Chartwell, home of Sir Winston Churchill. As we were walking around the room that housed all his insignias and badges, we noticed a gold one in the shape of a winkle shell. It was given by a coastal town and was marked 'Order of the Winkle'.

Behind us was a family — mum, dad and two small boys. Mum was reading out and pointing to all the badges and said, 'This is the order of the Winkle.' The smallest boy, in a loud voice, said, 'My winkle doesn't look like that!'

Pat Sherwin

Bridesmaid blues

Recently my granddaughter Amelia was to be a bridesmaid and had been to the church for a rehearsal. On arriving home, her mother asked her if she had to walk down the aisle behind Uncle Dennis and Auntie Deryn.

'Yes,' was her reply, 'but they kept getting in my way!'

Rachel Heath

Married bliss

Many years ago, we were living in Swaziland in Africa. The small village we lived in did not have a nursery school, so all the children had to catch a bus in the morning for the seven-mile journey to school in the next village, returning just before lunch.

Our next door neighbours had a four-year-old called Russell. One day he came home from nursery school, smiling like the cat who'd got the cream. 'Mummy,' he announced, 'I'm married!'

'Oh yes, darling?' replied his mum.

'I kissed Valerie on the bus!'

'Well', said his mum, 'now you are married you'll have to leave home and set up house with Valerie, leave school and go to work to earn money, you won't be able to play in the sandpit…'

Russell's face was falling throughout this catalogue of horrors. When his mum paused for breath he was very quick to get in with: 'Mummy, I'm not married any more!'

Kate Piries

Spectators only

Just prior to the outbreak of war in 1939 our family went to India and my father joined the Indian Army. My mother told me about a conversation between myself and her. I was about five or six at the time.

Me: 'Mummy, I want to go back to England.'

Mummy: 'Well, Davy darling, you can't, because there's a war on and you could get killed.'

Me: 'Oh, it's all right Mummy, I won't go inside — I'll just stand by the gate and watch.'

David Macdonald

Traffic duty

When I was a serving police officer my son, then six, was asked at school to write what his Daddy did. He wrote: 'My Daddy's a policeman; he's on traffic. When a lorry overturns he sometimes brings stuff home.'

Anon

Animal magic

A young school teacher I knew had her first job teaching five-year-olds in the Scottish Highlands. On her first day, she thought she would see if the children knew about animals and she produced a set of pictures, starting with a sheep, asking if anyone knew what it was.

As she received no response, she showed them a picture of a pig – still no response. Then she showed them a picture of a cow and immediately a small boy's hand shot up. 'Yes?' she said, 'what is it then?' to which the boy replied, 'That's a Friesian, I think the pig's a Landrace and the sheep's a Wensleydale!'

Frank Dawson

The Terrible Twos 2

Bird feed

When my grandson, about four, was making friends with a new little boy at nursery, my daughter-in-law heard one of their conversations:

New boy: 'I have a penis, do you?'

My grandson: 'Yes, Mummy puts ours on the bird table.'

I think 'peanuts' is the clue here! SK

Marjorie S. Johnson

Hopping mad

My seven-year-old grandson Matthew is football mad. Recently, while practising his skills in the garden, his ball went into an adjoining field and he went after it.

Mum was alerted by frantic, hysterical screams as Matthew came hurtling back, full pelt. He was too distraught to explain what was wrong, except that it was to do with his trousers. Struggling with trainers as well as frantic child, Mum finally removed the offending trousers, which proceeded to jump around the kitchen floor.

Every attempt to investigate the wriggling trousers was met by louder and louder screams from Matthew. It had to be a snake — probably an adder.

Eventually in the safety of the garden, the trousers were lifted high and out plopped an enormous frog which blinked a bit and hopped away!

Sylvia H. Whitlock

Family tree

When Beccy, our granddaughter, was going through the terrible twos stage, she had great difficulty in comprehending the family tree any further than Mum and Dad. Aunts and uncles and even the Grandma/Grandpa relationship were not understood. I was treated very much as an intruder and wasn't even allowed to bring the milk in from the front porch, let alone put my arm around my daughter without all hell breaking loose!

One day, Grandma and I took Beccy into town to buy her some shoes. While in the shop, she took it into her head to lie down, spreadeagled on the carpet, and shout at the top of her voice: 'I am NOT your poppet!'

Roger Pike

Four star or pasteurised?

When my son Chris was four, we lived in Honiton, Devon. We were visiting the annual show and watching a demonstration of cow milking by machine.

Afterwards we asked Chris what his favourite thing in the show was and he said, 'Watching the men filling the cows with petrol.'

Beryl Neighbour

What flavour?

On Good Friday I was invited to the opening of the bowling green at Ashton Cricket Club with my friend's family, including her four-year-old grandson. During refreshments in the club afterwards, Jonathan was running around with a packet of crisps in his hand when one of the members stopped him in his tracks and asked, 'Jonathan, are those Doc Martens?' to which he replied, 'No — they're cheese and onion.'

Joyce Lees

Spell check

A little boy at school asked me how to spell 'TOFFA'.

'What do you mean, Nick?' I asked.

'Well, I've got the Chris — I just need the 'topher'.

Iris Henesy-Lar

The Terrible Twos 2

Bowled over

One morning at breakfast, Holly, my three-year-old granddaughter, balanced a cereal bowl on her head and said, 'Grandma, I've got a bowl on my 'ead.'

Being an ex-schoolteacher, I replied, 'Holly, there's an H on head,' to which she retorted, 'No Grandma, it's a bowl!'

Stephanie Pettit

Doctor in the house

Many years ago, when the 'gooseberry bush' was still an acceptable excuse, I decided to be an enlightened mum, so told my two little daughters that the baby was growing in my tummy until it was big enough to be born.

'How will it get out?' demanded four-year-old Caroline.

'Oh,' I said hastily, 'the doctor will bring it out.' I was relieved when no other questions followed, but some months later Caroline came into my bedroom when I was undressed.

'What's that,' she asked, pointing to my vastly increased figure.

'I told you, darling — the baby is growing in there.'

She gave me a thoughtful look, then said, 'Is the doctor in there too?'

Olive Charters

Tiger feet

One day I was having a telephone conversation with my grandson, Jon Paul, aged five. I asked him what he had been doing and he told me that they had been learning to do Tiger Dancing at school.

Me: 'What's Tiger Dancing?'

Jon Paul: 'Well, you all stand in a straight line and do dancing and pretend to be a cowboy.'

Me: 'Do you mean line dancing?'

Jon Paul: 'Oh yes, I always get lions and tigers mixed up.'

Carol O'Brien

Ticked off

Some years ago, I went to the Aquashow in Bournemouth with my husband. There was some very spectacular diving being performed by some magnificent specimens of manhood.

As they were performing some rather daring acrobatics on the end of a 30-foot high diving board, I could not bear to look and put my hand over my eyes. A rather nice-looking little blonde boy, about seven, was sitting next to me. He gave me a nudge and said, in broad northern tones, 'Well, if yer dorn't laark it, yer shunt a cum.'

Marjorie Ross

Perturbed postie

I once opened the door to a very embarrassed postman. My son, Lee, had been posting sanitary towels to him through the letterbox, laughing delightedly as postie shoved them back through!

Wendy Berriman

Communion clout

When my daughter Vicki was about three, she went to her first Family Communion. She was taken to the altar rail for a blessing. Returning to our seats, she asked, in a loud indignant voice, 'What did I do wrong?' I replied, 'You didn't do anything wrong, darling.'

'Well, why did he hit me on the head then?'

Beryl Chiswell

Bungee challenge

A lady with whom I was working told me that she had taken her little girl, aged eight, along to see Starlight Express. Their conversation before the lights went down was:

'Well, would you do a bungee jump?'

'No, not until I was older.'

'How old?'

'Oh, about 90. That way, if I was to die, I wouldn't be missing much.'

John Wheater

The Terrible Twos 2

Tattoo trouble

My son once encountered a very heavily-tattoed man. He tutted, saying: 'Your Mum's gonna go mad when she sees you!'

'Why?' asked the bemused man.

'Because my Mum says, "I don't care what you draw — just keep the felt pens on the paper!"'

Natalie Durell

Dead comfy

My son and his family had been to a funeral and on their way back stayed with us for a few days. One morning my grandson, Christopher, then about five years old, climbed into bed with me and asked, 'Nan, you know when you die — do you come back to life again?' I said that no, I was afraid not and he replied, 'Well, you must be very comfortable in that box!'

Peggy Camp

Five thousand... to one

My daughter Lynda was at Sunday School and they were being told the story of Jesus feeding the five thousand. All the children were asked to draw a picture. The Sunday School teacher, on looking through the pictures, saw that Lynda had drawn only one person being fed by Jesus.

When the teacher asked her where all the other people were, she replied, 'They got fed up waiting and went home!'

Marianne Fowle

Eye-opener

A couple of years ago when my grandson Ben was four, he was sitting on my knee and we were having a gran/grandson heart-to-heart. We were looking deeply into each other's eyes.

'Oh Gran,' he breathed, 'I do love the way the triangles under your eyes fit just exactly into your glasses.'

Mary Good

Headless coffee

When we were children, my little brother 'Boo' was always tagging along after me and my twin sister. On one occasion, my sister and I were playing Scrabble with my father, when in trundles little brother:

Boo: 'I want to play, can I play, what are you playing, please let me play!'

Nadia: 'You can't play — you're not old enough.'

Boo *(lip trembling):* 'I am old enough!'

Me: 'You're not old enough — you can't spell long words.'

Boo: 'Can!'

Me: 'Can't!'

Boo: 'Can!'

Me: 'OK, you can play if you tell us the meaning of the word 'decapitated'.

His face lit up and he announced: 'It's a type of coffee!'

Talya

Eggs-asperating

My son Richard, then aged three, was collecting eggs with my Mother from the poultry arks in the orchard. On this particular day, the hens had not laid many eggs and Mum said, 'We aren't doing very well today, are we Richard?'

He gave the hens a really disgusted look and said, 'What's the matter with the buggers?'

Mum had a terrible time trying not to laugh, as she knew that was one of my father's expressions!

Penny Cartwright

"HOW DOES HE EXPECT US TO LAY
IF HE TALKS TO US LIKE THAT?"

The Terrible Twos 2

Private and confidential

When my son Michael was about four, we were out shopping in the supermarket and passed the counter with tampons. 'Mummy, what's in those boxes?' he asked. I told him that those are for ladies, they are private and not for children. No more was said.

A couple of weeks later, we were passing the same counter and he said, 'Mummy, I know what's in those boxes anyway — they are those things you poke your ears out with!'

Anon

In stitches

I had my two children by caesarian section and, while in the bath shortly after the birth of Joanne, her two-and-a-half-year-old brother Christopher wandered into the bathroom and stared at the scar on my tummy.

'Mummy,' he said, 'was that the zip you opened to get me out?' If only it were that easy!

Pam James

Talk back

My friend woke up her son for his second day at school, but he said it was a waste of time going again. When she asked him why, he said, 'Because I can't write, I can't read and the teacher won't let me talk!'

Gail Ditchfield

Rusty gran

My niece Deborah was at the 'Why?' stage where everything was questioned. We were walking past an old wire fence that was different colours in places where it had aged.

'Why's that fence a funny colour?' she asked. I told her that it was old and had gone rusty. She thought for a moment and then said, 'But Nanny's old and she's not rusty.'

Susan Harvey

Milky mistake

My little grandson Cameron, three and a half, lives in Singapore with his parents. One evening his mother said to him, 'Oh Cameron, I forgot to give you your milk today!' He walked across the room with a loud mutter: 'Stupid!'

Seeing red, his Mum said, 'Cameron, what did you say to me?' and he answered, 'I wasn't talking to you — I was talking to myself!'

Molly Barden

Loo queue

Jonathan *(aged eight):* 'Mummy, I've just realised why boys have willies and girls don't.'
Mummy: 'Oh, why is that then?'
Jonathan: 'Well, if we were all the same, just think how long the queues would be at the toilets!'

Anon

The Terrible Twos 2

On the scrap heap

Recently, I was showing my grandson, Nicholas, who is two and a half, some family photographs.

'And this, Nicholas, is a picture of my Mummy and Daddy.'

'Your Mummy and Daddy, Grandma?'

'Yes, darling.'

'Where are your Mummy and Daddy now, Grandma?'

'Well, they were very old, so they're not around any more.'

'Oh, I suppose you had to take them to the dump.'

Sonja Spechko

Flying saucer

One day my grandson Jamie, aged four, was upstairs having a pretend tea party with some friends, complete with plastic cups and saucers. Suddenly Stephanie came downstairs crying, so my son asked her what was wrong.

'Jamie threw a cup at me.'

'Jamie, why did you throw a cup at Stephanie?'

'Because I missed her with the saucer.'

Pat Connolly

Keep out!

When our elder son Ashley was about three, I used to tie the double gates at the end of the driveway together to prevent him from straying onto the road.

One day when I was doing this, he said, 'I know why you do that, Mummy.'

'Do you, darling?' I asked.

'Yes — to keep the neighbours out.'

Ann Jones

Daddy says

My grandson Charlie, aged four, met an elderly friend recently who was surprised by how much he had grown.

'Hello Charlie, you're growing into a proper little man.'

He replied, 'No I'm not, I'm a little git — Daddy said so.'

Patricia Coleman

Exercise book

The day my 'baby', Angharad, started full-time school was a very emotional one for me. She couldn't wait to get there, but I felt very tearful. After I left her, I went home, wept buckets and then thought I'd better get cracking to fill in the time until 3.15 pm.

I took the dog for a long walk and spring-cleaned the whole house, then started to get ready to pick her up. When the children filed out of the classroom, Angharad was near the front, one sock up and one down, looking rather tired but happy. I managed to restrain myself from bombarding her with questions until we got home, then I asked her what she had done during the day.

'Things,' was the answer. 'Oh, and we played outside three times and had a story before we came home.' I pressed a little further, 'Did you do any painting or sums or reading?' 'No!' came the answer. After a brief pause, she said, 'Miss Tiplady gave me a book and wrote my name on the front of it.' 'Oh,' I said, 'an exercise book.' 'No, silly', was the reply, 'it doesn't exercise — you write things down in it!'

Sally Howe

Sad Mary

My granddaughter Holly, aged four and a half, was really into the Christmas story during her first term at 'big' school. Quite the little artist, she was always drawing pictures of the Nativity scene. One such drawing depicted Mary, Joseph, baby Jesus and so forth.

'What a lovely picture!' exclaimed her mother. 'The colours are so good too. But why has Mary got such a sad face?'

'Because Jesus was a baby boy and she really wanted a girl!'

Janette Stewardson

The Terrible Twos 2

Furry fruit

When Michael, my grandson, was about six, he was was at my house one day and seemed totally fascinated by the contents of the fruit bowl. Thinking he had spotted a creepy-crawly scurrying about, I said to him, 'What's the matter Michael, is there something wrong with the fruit?'

He picked out a peach and replied, 'Nan, we don't have fur coats on our apples like you do.'

Olga Brace

Starry, starry night

My husband died when my grandson was two years old. My daughter-in-law did a wonderful job of explaining what had happened to Grandad Frank, to which Christopher exclaimed: 'Well, I think he's gone to be a star, that bright one there!'

Some time later, my mother died and it was decided that she'd gone to be a star with Grandad Frank. A few months later when Christopher was staying with me, a very close family friend died and I was debating whether I should tell him or leave it to his mother to explain. As we were meeting up with a lot of other family members during the day, who would obviously be upset and talking about it, I decided it was best to tell him and explained that Margery had been very poorly and had gone to be a star with Grandad Frank and Nanny Dos.

Christopher gave a big sigh and shrugged his shoulders, saying, 'At this rate we'll be able to read our book in bed without the light on.'

Joy Worral

Woolly present

Some friends of ours, Bill and Jan, asked their son Sam what he would like for his fifth birthday. Without hesitation he said, 'Buzz Lightyear and Woody,' from the film *Toy Story*.

Bill and Jan went to check the prices at the local toy shop and, realising that they were quite expensive, said to Sam, 'We think it would be too much for Mummy and Daddy to buy you both, so we'll get one and Grandma will get you the other.'

The disappointed expression on Sam's face prompted them to ask him what was wrong. He turned round with a very sad face and said, 'I don't want a knitted one.'

Martyn Preston

Hungry mum

When my sons were about two and four, I overheard this conversation:

Philip *(the elder):* 'I've got a willy.'

Pause.

Philip: 'You've got a willy.'

Pause.

Philip: 'Babies have got willies.'

Another pause. Richard was listening intently, but playing at the same time.

Philip: 'Daddy's got a willy.'

Richard: 'What's Mummy got?'

Philip *(after a long pause):* 'Mummy's got an appetite!'

Graham A. Pavey

Not this time!

My daughter had great difficulty in telling the time and John at the corner shop used to help her. He had a broken old clock and every afternoon when she went to spend her 5p, he would set the hands to a different time and she had to tell him what time it was before she was served.

She must have had a bad afternoon one day, because she marched up to the counter, slapped her 5p on the glass top and shouted, 'Give me some sweets and I don't care what bloody time it is!'

Wendy Berriman

The Terrible Twos 2

Keep off the grass

After I was divorced, my children came to see me one weekend. My house had a long garden with other houses backing onto the side of it. My daughter Emma looked at one of the semi's adjoining the side and said: 'Dad, why has that man got half his house in someone else's garden?'

Vernon L. Phillips

Walk don't jump

Sarah, nearly three at the time, loved jumping into puddles. We were going to a wedding dressed in our best clothes. Daddy lifted her out of the car and, spotting temptation nearby, said, 'Sarah, do *not* jump in that puddle!'
Needless to say, Sarah went straight in.
'What did I say?' shouted her Daddy.
'But Daddy, you said, "Don't jump in that puddle" — I didn't, I walked!'

Shirley Brown

Baby exchange

When my son John was two years old and his sister was a baby, we discovered that I was expecting again. My husband and I thought that we should break the news to him early to get him used to the idea.
'John, how would you like another little brother or sister?'
'Well,' he said, after a little thought and a pause, 'I know she's quite naughty, but I'd quite like to keep her!'

Vicki Baxter

Boy or girl?

My daughter, son-in-law and grandchildren Thomas, six, and Faye, four, were all watching a television programme in which a baby was born. The nurse held the baby up and said to the parents, 'Congratulations, you have a beautiful little girl!'
Thomas: 'How do they know it's a girl when nobody has bought her a dress?'
Mum: 'What have you got that Faye hasn't?'
Thomas *(after some thought):* 'A bigger bedroom and a Buzz Lightyear.'

Brian Baker

Bottoms up

We were living in Scotland at the time, and I was having a home visit from the local Church of England minister. The best china was out and I handed the minister a cup of tea and Stephen, my two-year-old, a cup of orange juice. 'What do you say?' I said, awaiting his usual 'thank you.'

He smiled, raised his cup and said, 'Cheers!'

Marion A. Thomson

Frisco disco

When my grandson Andrew was four, he came home from nursery school and told my daughter, Debbie, that his best friend was going to a disco for a week.

'A disco for a week?' repeated Debbie, 'Are you sure?'

'Yes,' said Andrew, 'that's what he told me.'

Some days later Debbie saw the best friend's Mum and said, 'What's this I hear about you all going off to a disco for a week?'

'A disco for a week?' said the bemused Mum. After a short pause, 'No, no. We're all going off to San Francisco for a week!'

Janet Wilson

Glamorous mum

War had just broken out and it was a dull, rainy day in Norwich where I was born. I was then two years old and my mother was at a loss what to do with me, so she decided to risk taking me to the cinema. The film was 'Goodbye Mr Chips', starring Robert Donat and Greer Garson.

I was mesmerised by the entire scene and atmosphere and, during a moment of high drama, a beautifully permanently-waved blonde Greer Garson appeared on the screen and a little voice piped up: 'Oh, I wish I had a mummy like that!'

There was a ripple of laughter throughout the cinema and my mother was eternally grateful for the darkness to hide her embarrassment!

Ann Marriott

Toothy problem

I was a child of the '50s and have crossed bottom teeth, as my dentist wasn't trained to deal with braces. On one occasion, the daughter of a colleague was sitting on my knee and had a bird's eye view of my teeth. After thinking quietly, she said, 'Maureen, are you cutting new teeth?' I was 40 at the time!

Maureen Kamitsis

Leg warmer

My granddaughter Victoria, then almost three, was watching me put on my tights and suddenly said, 'You've got lovely legs, Granny Sammy.' I was surprised, as I've always considered my blue-veined legs to be one of my worst features. I was flattered, until she added, 'They've got such pretty patterns on them!'

Sandra Goodchild

Little angel

When our youngest child, Ben, was four, we decided to apply for a place in the local Catholic First School. The day arrived for Ben and us to have a guided tour of the school and to meet 'Sister', the Headmistress, so that Ben's suitability for a place could be assessed.

She sat resplendant looking every inch a nun. A crucifix hung on the wall behind her large desk. Ben sat on his Daddy's lap looking very angelic and perfectly behaved. All went well until the Headmistress leant forward and, in soft Irish tones, asked, 'Now Benjamin, are you a good boy?'

'Oh, yes,' he said with deep sincerity, 'but sometimes I'm very naughty because I make marks in my knickers.'

Karen Hunt

Holiday luggage!

When our two boys were one and three I was taking them to visit their Nan. On the way, a large car passed us with a bride and groom in the back. Grahame wanted to know where they were going, so I said, 'They are going on their honeymoon, which is a lovely holiday.'

Some time later a hearse passed us. 'Oh, look!' said Grahame, 'Those people are going on holiday and taking their wardrobe with them.'

M. Read

Wax-work

Granddaughter Ellie was nearly three when she came to a beauty parlour with my daughter and I. It had rained heavily. Some time later, she was 'pretend reading' a little book by interpreting the pictures out loud. She started off: 'Well, it was a sunny day and the little girl went out to play in the garden.'

She turned over the page and continued, 'But when it was raining, she had to go indoors to … to … to …' — we waited while she thought of something — 'to have her legs waxed!'

Audrey J. Corke

Off colour

Several years ago, I decided to take my young cousin, then aged about six, to the theatre. He'd never been before, so I took great pains to tell him all about the production he was going to see, and how it would be very different from the telly.

He seemed to grasp the fact that it would all be happening live in front of him and I was confident that I'd instilled some enthusiasm for seeing his first live theatre show. We walked through the foyer and the usherette took our tickets. Just as we were about to take our seats in the large auditorium, a young voice asked the usherette: 'Will it be in colour or black and white?'

Robert Cope

Fed up

One day I was looking after my granddaughter Ciara, aged nine. She had to finish some homework before Easter where she had to stick the appropriate verse below the correct picture of Jesus on the cross and the Feast of the Passover. Getting rather irritated while doing this, she said, 'I am not going to be a Christian when I grow up — it's too boring!'

Nanny Shirley Evans

Large gift

Our daughter and son-in-law were taking our two grandsons Liam, five, and Niall, three, on holiday.

'Where are you going on holiday?' I asked.

'Corfu,' said Niall.

'Where is that?'

'Greece,' he replied.

Stretching my arms out wide, I said, 'When you come back I want a present this big.'

After a short pause, Niall chirped, 'I'll bring you a newspaper!'

Sandra and Tony Graham

Graveyard gaffe

The builders in our church were causing havoc, so we had to take the little ones out and alongside to use the toilets. There's a large cemetery opposite and on this trip, one child said, 'What's that big park over there with all the rocks in it?'

Jacky Wright

Cowboy gait

My husband Jim had a vasectomy when my son James was two and a half years old, and was extremely brave about the whole thing. After being 'done', he managed to drive the car home and decided to take it easy for a few days.

Consequently, Jim and James were able to play Cowboys and Indians together, one of James' favourite games. When I came home from work the following day, James asked me, 'Mummy, why is Daddy walking like a cowboy?'

Jan Parkin

"BUT DADDY, YOU'RE SUPPOSED TO BE AN INDIAN ! "

The Terrible Twos 2

Grassy dad

Many years ago when our son Shaun was about three, we had a hard day in the garden, weeding, cutting the privet hedges and mowing the lawn, with Shaun helping. As I was sweaty and grimy, I decided I would have a bath. I was lying there enjoying a soak, when into the bathroom came Shaun and stood staring at me for what seemed like ages.

Eventually, he said, 'Dad, when I am a big man will I be covered in grass like you are?'

Terry and Christine Flaherty

Side salad

When my second daughter Erin was two days old, I developed mastitis and the midwife suggested the old trick of cabbage leaves in the bra. It was late on Sunday afternoon so cabbages were none too easy to come by, but eventually we got one from a friend. My husband was despatched to collect it and I duly stuffed a leaf into my bra.

An hour or so later, Erin demanded a feed. As I tried to get myself organised with cushions and a drink of water, Erin was screaming and Freja, my two-year-old, was talking to her. I removed the now almost cooked cabbage leaf and Freja said, 'All right, all right, Erin — it's coming and you've got salad with it!'

Amanda Brown

Follow-my-leader

When our granddaughter Olivia was two, my husband (whom she calls Pappa) and I went on holiday with our daughter, her husband, Olivia and baby Cassie. We had a marvellous time, taking over from the parents to give them a break whenever possible and thoroughly enjoyed spending two weeks with the children.

After we returned, Olivia was listening to a news item on stalkers one day. She asked her mother what a stalker was and, without going into lurid detail, our daughter explained that it was someone who followed you everywhere, and was always there whatever you did. Olivia interrupted, saying, 'Oh, yes, yes, just like Pappa and Grandma in Portugal!'

Barbara Jaquis

Room service

One weekend my husband and I decided to visit Hadrian's Wall and took our son Peter, then six, with us. After a day of walking we returned to the hotel and Peter had his tea and was safely esconced in his own room adjoining ours. We heard a knock on Peter's door. Thinking that someone had got the wrong room, we went into the corridor to see who it was.

A waiter from room service was going into Peter's room with a trolley laden with a three-course meal!

'You must have made a mistake,' I said to the waiter. 'No, madam,' said the waiter, 'Room 8, Peter Kell — he's just called room service and ordered dinner.' So my husband and I went into Peter's room with the waiter to see him lounging on the bed watching TV.

'It's OK, Mum,' he said, 'I've seen them do it on TV. All you do is pick up the phone and tell them what you want and they bring it — and it's free!'

Patricia Kell

The Terrible Twos 2

Veggie nightmare

My granddaughters Vikki and Jodie come to stay with me every other weekend. As we sat down to lunch one day, Jodie, then five, started to cry. When I asked what was wrong, Vikki, munching her sausages, said, 'She's frightened.' Jodie sobbed even louder. 'Why,' I asked, giving her a hug.

'Oh, Nanny,' she cried, 'I had some vegetarian sausages at my friend's house the other day, and now I'm really frightened because I keep thinking I might become a vegetarian!'

Joan V. Griffin

Electric shock

My son, Gareth, when he was nearly three, used to sit on the toilet and in a sing-song voice would call out, 'Please will you come and wipe my bottom, please will you come and wipe my bottom…' until someone went to sort him out.

On the day in question, Gareth had not long been dealt with and was at the front door with me, when the loud booming voice of my husband Keith sounded down the stairs, 'Please will you come and wipe my bottom, please will you come and wipe my bottom,' in imitation of Gareth.

Unbeknown to Keith, I had opened the door to the electricity man who had come to read the meter and he was standing there with a 'look' I will never forget. To make matters worse, what I said next did not make the situation any easier, as I turned to him and said, 'That's my husband,' to which he replied, 'Yes, madam,' and was out of the door like a shot. Funnily enough, I haven't seen him since!

Sheelah Evans

Shepherd's pie

Granny to grandson Myles, aged four, during a conversation about sheep:
'Do you know what shepherds do?'
He thought seriously for a moment, then said, 'They make pies!'

Joan Aartsen

Buy two, get one free

My husband Kris and I are the proud parents of two sets of twins. When the youngest, Zak and Dee, were four, I had to take them to the local hospital for a check-up.

As we were sitting in the waiting area, I got talking to a woman who was very heavily pregnant. She told me she was expecting triplets.

I could see Zak listening very intently to our conversation and sensed that he was about to say something profound. Stupidly, I asked him what was troubling him.

Very quietly, he whispered, 'Mummy, what are triplets?' I explained. He immediately responded loudly with: 'Next time you and Daddy have babies, you can order two and get one free like this lady!'

Kath O'Brien

Deflated dad

Some friends of ours have three children and one day when they were small, Isa had had enough of the screaming chaos and told Pete to take them out for a while. It was a dark, depressing Sunday morning in November. Pete sighed as he looked at the rain lashing against the window and wished that he didn't have to go out.

Nevertheless, he helped the three tots one by one into their wellies, jumpers, waterproofs and rain hats.

Finally, just as he opened the front door to lead them all out, a voice piped up from Ellie, the oldest, 'Daddy, I want a wee-wee.'

Pete was speechless and glowered at her, but before he had time to say anything, she continued, 'I know, Daddy, and you've just put my bloody coat on!'

Simon Dawson and Thelma Brewster

Switching signs

When our son was about six, we were travelling through Suffolk on our way to Essex. From the back of the car he suddenly said, 'Dad, where is One P Switch?'

He had seen a sign for Ipswich!

Anon

The Terrible Twos 2

Wine-tasting!

My granddaughter Georgina Mae was told by her parents that a baby brother or sister would be arriving, but at present it was in Mummy's tummy. Georgina replied, 'Daddy has wine in *his* tummy!'

Anon

On-line Jesus

Stephania was listening to an adult conversation about the impact of the Millenium Bug.

Stephania: 'Grandpa, what's a Millenium Bug?'

Me: 'It's a problem that might affect the way in which computers tell the time after the Millenium, which may mean that some of them will go wrong.'

Stephania: 'What's the Millenium?'

Me: 'It's 2000 years since Jesus was born and happens at the end of next year.'

Stephania: 'Oh, so Jesus was into computers?'

Anthony D. Humphries

Potato feast

Some years ago my sister came to visit to show off her new baby. My wife was at home with our four-year-old, James, and after a while my sister indicated discreetly that it was time to breastfeed the infant.

My wife took James firmly by the hand and said, 'Let's go into the kitchen and make a nice cup of tea.' Sensing that something was going on that he should know about, James dodged his Mum and ran back into the lounge. However, he returned to the kitchen in double-quick time, wide-eyed and blurted out: 'Mummy! Mummy! The baby's eating a potato!'

G. Edwards

God in Devon

When Jenny was about three, she seemed to be a little confused about the difference between theology and geography. While driving along one day, a little enquiring voice came from the back of the car, 'Daddy, why do people that die go to Devon?'

Alan Watmore

Panto elephant

Rachel, now eleven, was attending a rather posh school in Cambridge. Each child in her class was to have a part in the Christmas pantomime and Rachel was to be a toy elephant.

It took some time to attach both tail and trunk and it must all have been getting too much for her as, a couple of days before 'curtain up', she was sitting at the dinner table, chin in hands and declared in a very disgruntled voice, 'I'm sick of being a bleeding elephant!'

Kathleen Thompson

Get plastered!

A little fellow knocked on my office door amidst sniffs and sobs, and said: 'I've caught my willy in my zip.'

I went straight into teacher mode and said, 'Oh, my dear, let me see what we can do to make it better — we need a plaster.'

'I've already got a plaster,' he sobbed.

'Did you get it from one of the other teachers?' I asked.

'No, I've taken the plaster off my verruca and stuck it on my willy.'

Iris Henesy-Lar

Mistaken tortoise

My son and his family were staying with us one weekend and Andrew was in the shower. His son Paul wandered in and started to chat.

Paul: 'You've got a bigger tortoise than me, haven't you Daddy?'

Rather nonplussed and wondering what was coming next, Andrew pretended he hadn't heard properly.

Andrew: 'What did you say, Paul?'

Paul repeated the question but Dad was still in the dark.

Andrew: 'Point it out to me.'

Paul solemnly pointed to his Dad's chest and Andrew realised he was trying to say 'torso'!

Catherine R. Thomas

Where there's a will ...

A couple of years ago my daughter was bathing her children Aaron, then seven, and Rachel, then two. My daughter was drying Aaron and Rachel caught sight of his 'bits'.

'What's that?' she asked.

'That's my willy,' said Aaron.

'I want one,' she said. My daughter explained that little girls don't have willies, but Rachel was still adamant.

Downstairs later on, Rachel went to the paper rack and got out the Argos catalogue. My daughter had asked the children to have a look through it for some ideas for Christmas presents.

'What are you looking for, Rachel?' asked my daughter.

'A willy,' came the reply.

Yvonne Reeves

First Aid?

Rebecca, aged eight, is a very new and enthusiastic Brownie.

Rebecca *(In the bath, scrubbing away at a tiny scratch on her leg):* 'Gran, I must get this very clean to make sure there aren't any germs in it, 'cos that's what they teach us in First Aid.'

Me: 'What else do you learn in First Aid? When I was a Girl Guide we learnt how to put someone's arm in a sling.'

Rebecca: 'No, we don't do that, but we learn lots of other things — I can even do mouth-to-mouth suffocation!'

Joan Shead

French letters

Our daughter and son-in-law decided to go on holiday to France with our two grandchildren, Elizabeth and Jordan. Jordan, being the older child, wanted to know everything, so they decided to teach him a few basic words in French. So the first word he got his tongue round was 'Yes', being 'Wee' in French. After mastering this word, they asked him what he thought the French for 'No' was. After a long think, he said, 'Poo.'

Grandad Jim T.

Pleased to meet you

While busy in our front garden, I became aware that a small boy from a few houses away was standing quietly watching me. 'Hello, Hugh, how are you?'

'Fine,' he replied, 'I think you know my Mum and Dad.'

'Yes, Hugh, I do.'

'Well,' said Hugh, 'I'm their son.'

Doug

Mucky bunny

Three-year-old Charlotte told me: 'Uncle Steve's got a dirty rabbit!' Looking to her mother for enlightenment, I was told, 'Uncle Steve's got a dirty habit — he smokes!'

Margaret Rossall

Toilet trouble

When my daughter Catherine was two and a half, we were staying at a very basic caravan site in Wales and I was bathing her in a big butler sink in the ladies toilets. A woman came in and went into a cubicle and was obviously having a little 'trouble' judging by the funny noises coming from that direction.

I held my breath, dreading a comment from Catherine, but she said nothing and I relaxed. Some minutes later, the woman came out and crossed over to the basins. Before I could do anything, Catherine smiled sweetly at the woman and said, 'I heard your bottom talk!'

Sheelah Evans

Linguistically gifted

Our grandson Kieran, aged four, was chattering away to us and I thought he sounded as if he might be coming down with something.

Me: 'Have you got a cold, Kieran?'
Kieran: 'No, why?'
Me: 'I thought you sounded a little husky.'
Kieran: 'I can speak any language.'

Marie E. Simmons

Bed and breakfast

We had some friends to stay and, in order to accommodate everyone, the parents were to sleep in our room, their teenage son was to have our three-year-old daughter's room, while she went back to her cot for a week. The son agreed to pay her a sixpence for every night he slept in her room,

When the visit was over, we went to a large, crowded store to buy her a much-desired doll with the three shillings and sixpence. Purchase complete, she said loudly, 'Come on, Mummy — let's go and spend yours. How much did Uncle Ron pay you to sleep in your bed?'

Anon

Jack, Queen, King

I was trying on a dress in a shop cubicle with husband and three-year-old Lucy waiting outside.

Assistant: 'Hello, I have a grandson about your size. How old are you?'

Lucy: 'Three.'

Assistant: 'When is your birthday?'

Lucy: 'Um, January.'

Assistant: 'So is my grandson's. What date is yours?'

Lucy looked thoughtful and mutely appealed to Dad for help.

Dad: 'What comes after ten?'

Lucy *(triumphantly to Assistant):* 'Jack.'

Guess how we taught her to count?

Anon

Royal stuffing

I took my five-year-old granddaughter to the National Railway Museum in York and showed her the splendid collection of Royal railway coaches from the start of royal transport to the present day. Looking through the window of Queen Victoria's coach, which included a full-size wax-work of her majesty reclining on a couch, I explained who she was.

On another visit with a small friend of hers, my granddaughter led the way and explained what everything was, now she was an 'expert'. Arriving at Queen Victoria's coach, she informed her friend, 'This is Queen Victoria — when she died they stuffed her and put her in here!'

D.E. Bowerman

A load of tripe

One day we were having tripe for lunch and my young son had never had it before. I noticed he wasn't eating his lunch and asked, 'Don't you like it, darling?'

'No,' he said, tears running down his face. 'I hate flannel — I'd rather have a piece of bread and bugger.'

Ellen

Foxy passion

Many years ago, we were watching a wildlife programme about urban foxes with our two young boys, Sean and Simon. The narrator was saying that the naturally reserved male threw all caution to the wind in spring, following the vixen everywhere she went, day and night, until the right moment arrived for passion.

The moment arrived in broad daylight, right in the middle of a suburban garden. Although we considered ourselves open-minded, my wife and I  grew more embarrassed by the second as the boys, aged five and eight, sat glued to the set, as foxy emotions grew to a fevered pitch, with much grunting from the male and terminating in a piercing scream from the vixen.

We all sat, motionless and dumbstruck, for what was a long, uncomfortable ten seconds or so, when Simon, the youngest, turned to face us and asked, 'Does that mean they're married now, Daddy?'

Doug Watts

Cash or card?

Charlotte and I were playing shop one day and, after she'd brought me several things, I said, 'I'll just get some money to pay you.' Whereupon Charlotte, quick as a flash, replied, 'It's all right, Granny — I'll take your card!'

Margaret Rossall

Ooh, ahh, Lineker!

On our holiday to Spain with our son Gavin, we spent a day in Barcelona. Back at school, Gavin, then seven, was invited by the Headmaster to tell his classmates about his holiday. On his tour of Barcelona, he reported that he'd seen the football stadium, visited the zoo and, as an afterthought said, 'Oh, and we saw the statue of Christopher Columbus.'

The Headmaster said, 'Can you remember what Christopher Columbus is famous for?'

Gavin replied, 'Is he the man who brought Gary Lineker to Barcelona?'

Margaret Newbrook

Off with her head!

My husband and I were on holiday in Malta with our two grandchildren James, eight, and Sarah, ten.

Sarah: 'What churches are there on Malta, Nan?'

Me: 'Catholic, Sarah.'

Sarah: 'I'm Catholic, aren't I, Nan?'

Me: 'Yes, darling.'

James: 'I am too, aren't I, Nan?'

Me: 'No, James, you're Church of England.'

I tried to explain all about Henry the Eighth and the differences between Catholic and C of E as briefly as I could.

Sarah: 'So it means that James can get a divorce?'

Me: 'Yes, that's right.'

Sarah: 'Well, what about me, Nan?'

James: 'You have your head cut off, doesn't she, Nan?'

Anon

Footnote

Rachel, aged five, called to show me her new shoes and, once they had been admired, I asked her what size shoes she now took.

'The same size as my feet, of course!' was the reply.

Sue Graham

Oi you!

My son Christopher came home from school at the end of his first year and said he'd had his name called out in assembly by the Headmaster, but he didn't know why. As he is a sensitive and well-behaved boy, we wondered what had happened.

Me: 'Had you been talking in assembly?'

Christopher: 'No.'

Me: 'Were you near someone who was talking? Maybe Mr Brown made a mistake?'

Christopher: 'No, I don't think so.'

Me: 'Had you done some specially good work?'

Christopher: 'Mr Brown didn't say so.'

Me: 'What could it be then? Are you sure you weren't naughty'

Christopher: 'Oh, no — I wasn't naughty. Mr Brown called out my name. When you're naughty he calls you "Oi!" '

Adrian Moore

Helping hand

I offered to take my two grandchildren to the park as their Mum and Dad wanted to clear out the garage. Off I went with Joseph, aged five, with his roller skates and George, aged two and a half, with his bike. Before we went, I asked if they wanted to go to the toilet first. George, who was being toilet-trained, said yes, so I asked if he needed a hand. He said yes, so off we went to the toilet and then the park.

After spending a while on the swings and slides, we went home for lunch. By this time, I was bursting to go to the loo, which I mentioned to their Mum, when a little voice piped up, 'Do you need a hand?'

Pat Shirra

Booby prize

Kathryn, aged six, and Christopher, aged three, began arguing. The argument proceeded along the lines of:

'I go to school. *You* don't!'

'I've got a remote-control car. *You* haven't!'

'Well, *I've* got a Barbie typewriter!'

'So what! *I've* got a train set.'

This continued for a while until Kathryn had had enough. 'Well, anyway,' she declared, 'you're never getting any boobies!'

Julia V. Thompson

Vital statistics

The whole family, including Ben, seven, and Sophie, five, were looking forward to spending New Year's Day at our house. The children were particularly excited because our son Christopher, who was in the army, would also be there. Ben had been told that Christopher had a 48-inch chest and was looking forward to meeting a real-life Action Man!

The great day arrived and, during conversation, the subject of Christopher's chest size came up. He revealed that he had lost weight, so it was only 46 inches, to which Ben replied, 'That's only six inches bigger than yours, Mum.'

Anon

End of her tether

William, aged five, had been at school for just a few weeks when he came home one day and asked, 'Mummy, what is a tether?'

'Well,' I replied, 'it's something you use to tie up a goat or horse. Why do you ask?'

'Because my teacher, Mrs Morton, says that she is at the end of hers!'

Mary Guppy

The Terrible Twos 2

Quick cure

My great nephew Adam developed diabetes and the nurse at the hospital was giving him his injection. He was getting upset about the needle, so the nurse comforted him by saying, 'Don't worry, Adam — by the time I die they will have found a cure for your trouble.'

A few days later, his Daddy was administering the injection when Adam said, 'Dad, when is that nurse going to die?'

Doris Langley

Decimal fairies

My son Julian was losing his baby teeth at the time decimal currency started. He had already lost a couple of teeth and the tooth fairies had given him an old shilling (five pence) for each one.

As I put him to bed one night, he put another tooth under his pillow and said, 'I hope the fairies give me one of those seven-sided coins this time.'

Maureen Martin

Too old to party?

I look after my grandson, Harry, three times a week. Nearly three, he realised that when Granny comes, Mummy, Daddy and sister Amy all go out, so I usually get greeted with: 'You go home, Granny!'

When I arrived one Saturday, I got the same greeting. 'But I've come to Amy's party.' I said. He gave me a look and replied, 'But you're too old!'

Ruth Green

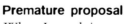

Premature proposal

When I was doing my teacher training and was a mere eighteen years old, I was on playground duty one day when a little boy called Sean proposed to me! Another little boy called Arron overheard and shouted, 'Don't be daft Sean, by the time you're old enough she'll be dead and gone!'

Sheelah Evans

Socket to me

After my son and his wife had their second child, I was called in to look after Katherine, aged four. She was playing happily by herself and, spotting a big pile of ironing, I thought I'd do something useful. I didn't want to use the wrong socket, so I called out to Katherine, 'Where does Mummy usually stand when she does the ironing?' There was a moment of silence and Katherine replied, 'She stands on the floor.'

Joan Easton

Bear necessity

When Katy was four we were watching a programme about bears.

Katy: 'Bears eat honey don't they, Mum?'

Me: 'Yes, and where does honey come from?'

Katy *(after a moment's thought):* 'Bees!'

Me: 'Very good. And where does milk come from?'

Katy *(with a scornful look):* 'Well, Tesco of course.'

Anon

Hide and seek

When Lesley was three I lost her in the house! I went through the usual 'Where are you hiding?' routine and 'Come out now', but there was silence. After a few minutes of searching, panic was setting in. Then I noticed a little figure in red on the other side of the glass front door. By this time I was in tears and opened the door and shouted, 'How did you get outside? I was worried about you!' Lesley was distressed too and said, through her sobs, 'But Mummy — *I* knew where I was!'

Anon

Facts of life

I was attempting a woman-to-woman chat with Naomi, nine, about the facts of life. After I'd tackled the 'mummy's' side of things, Naomi wanted to know how daddies were involved. I gave her a brief outline of what I felt she needed to know. She looked puzzled and said, 'Well, how come I never see any of this going on?'

Jenny Tyrie

Anyone at home?

I have a sweet six-year-old neighbour, but he thinks I need his company a lot more than I do. The other day when I saw him coming, I didn't answer the door. The next day he called again and said, 'I called yesterday but nobody answered the door,' so I said, 'I expect I was out shopping.' He replied, 'Well, I looked through your letterbox and I saw a lady with your clothes on.'

Vi Saunders

Holy brick!

My mother was a teacher at a local primary school, teaching four-year-olds. One religious instruction period, my mother asked her class, 'Now, children, what do we mean by "martyr"?' Young Brian, who was the son of a builder, replied: 'Please Miss, it's what me Dad puts between bricks.'

Simon Ilett

Heavenly gran

When my children were small we were very friendly with an Irish family. Both families being Catholic, we used to attend Sunday Mass together every week. My daughter Maria was friends with Josie, who was the same age and, one Sunday at church, Josie went over to light a candle. Maria asked her what she was doing. 'I'm lighting a candle for my Gran. She's in heaven,' explained Josie. Not wanting to be outdone, Maria said, 'Well, I'm going to light a candle for *my* Gran — she's in Enfield.'

Lynn Puertas

Dinner distress

When my son's third child was born, I went to stay with them to help look after Sophie, aged four, and Victoria, aged two. One day, I was preparing dinner when Sophie asked, 'What's for dinner, Nanna?' In all innocence, I replied, 'Bubble and squeak.'

Sophie immediately burst into tears and wouldn't be consoled. Her mother asked me what was wrong and when I told her, all became clear — Bubble and Squeak were the names of her guinea pigs!

Eileen Knight

The Terrible Twos 2

Acknowledgements
Special thanks are due to the contributors to
Sarah Kennedy's BBC Radio 2 programme who have given
permission for their letters to be included in this book.

Illustrators
Beccy Blake *pages 7, 12, 19, 25, 32, 37, 44, 51, 54, 60*
Martin Cater *pages 8, 14, 15, 18, 33, 42, 43, 45, 53, 59*
Chris Duggan *pages 11, 16, 23, 29, 34, 41, 47, 52, 57, 58*
Carol Pike *pages 10, 17, 21, 24, 27, 30, 35, 38, 48, 56*

Editor May Corfield
Designer Vicki Pacey
Project Editor Jaynie Senior